You Can Write

AWESOME

Stories

by Jennifer Fandel

Consultant:
Terry Flaherty, PhD
Professor of English
Minnesota State University, Mankato

CAPSTONE PRESS
a capstone imprint

First Facts is published by Capstone Press,
1710 Roe Crest Drive, North Mankato, Minnesota 56003.
www.capstonepub.com

Books published by Capstone Press are manufactured with paper
containing at least 10 percent post-consumer waste.

Library of Congress Cataloging-in-Publication Data
Fandel, Jennifer.
  You can write awesome stories / by Jennifer Fandel.
     p. cm. — (First facts. You can write)
  Includes index.
  Summary: "Introduces readers to the key steps in writing a fictional story through
the use of examples and exercises"—Provided by publisher.
  ISBN 978-1-4296-7615-1 (library binding)
  ISBN 978-1-4296-7960-2 (paperback)
  1. Fiction—Authorship—Juvenile literature. I. Title.
  PN3355.F27 2012
  808.3—dc23   2011035762

Editorial Credits
Jill Kalz, editor; Juliette Peters, designer; Kathy McColley, production specialist

Photo Credits
Dreamstime: Dpproductions, 17, Elena Butinova, 4, Ingvar Bjork, 12 (moose), Jiri Hera, 6 (pig),
Seow Ai Ti Angeline, 8 (boy), Tracy0703, 18; Shutterstock: Anat-oli, 3 (pig), 12 (pigs), 22 (both),
Andy Dean Photography, 21, Cindi Wilson, 6 (wagon), David Gilder, cover (girl), Erik Lam,
cover (iguana), fivespots, 8 (bird), James Deboer, 7 (turtle), Jon Slevec, 13, klohka, 15, Lisa F.
Young, 7 (clown), 24, Liudmila P. Sundikova, 6 (girl), Monkey Business Images, 5, 10, plazas
i subiros, 14, pr2is, 9, Racheal Grazias, 11, studio BM, 7 (robot), Taiga, 16 (right), Tomasz
Markowski, 19,wacpan, cover (pencil), xtrekx, 16 (left)

Artistic Effects
Shutterstock: Konstantin Sutyagin (balloons)

Printed in the United States of America in North Mankato, Minnesota.

062012   006828R

TABLE of CONTENTS

Tell Me a Story

Your classroom lizard was lost. But he was found when he jumped on your teacher's head.

The cat dreamed of playing the piano. He practiced every day and became famous.

Everyone tells stories. Some stories are true. Some are make-believe. Stories may teach a lesson. They may show you people and places you've never seen before. Or they may be just plain fun!

Exercise

Name three of your favorite stories, true or not. They may be written stories or ones told by friends or family. Why do you like these stories best? What makes each story special for you?

FAST FACT

Stories about make-believe people and events are called fiction. Stories about real people and events are called nonfiction.

Who Are You? CHARACTERS

Every story has at least one **character**. Characters are the people, animals, or creatures in a story.

Characters can be:
- the girl who dresses like a superhero.
- the pig that picks up trash in its red wagon.
- the uncle in a cowboy hat who tells jokes.

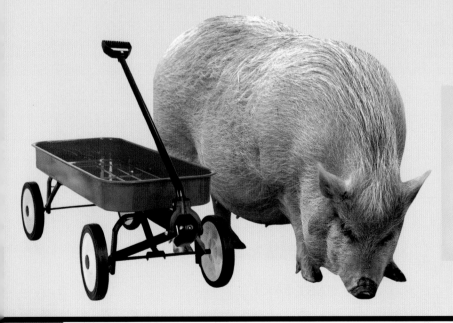

Main characters are the most important characters in a story. They speak and act more than others.

character—a person, animal, or creature in a story

Create three characters, and write a few sentences about each. Maybe you imagine a clown, a robot, and a turtle. Give each character a name.

What do your characters look like? Smell like? Sound like? How do they move? What do they like to do?

7

Exactly DETAILS

Details make sure readers understand your story. They help readers imagine how things look, smell, sound, taste, or feel. Details answer questions in readers' minds.

Instead of:
The boy had a pet.
Try:
Archie had a **chubby, one-eyed green** parrot named Orville.

Details help readers know which boy and what type of pet he owns. The boy now has a name. And readers learn what his bird, Orville, looks like.

detail—a fact about an object

FAST FACT

Words that describe people, places, or things are called adjectives. In the example, "chubby," "one-eyed," and "green" are adjectives. These words describe the parrot.

9

A Time and Place   SETTING

Every story happens sometime and somewhere. The **setting** tells readers when and where a story happens. Use your senses to make a place come alive.

Kids **packed** the cafeteria. Trays **CLATTERED**. The smell of fish sticks filled the room.

In this example, the setting is a crowded, noisy cafeteria. Because the room is full and smells like food, it's probably lunchtime.

setting—when and where a story happens

Exercise

Create a setting, such as an amusement park or zoo. Use your five senses. List the things you see when you walk through the gate. Is it daytime or nighttime? What time of year is it? What do you hear? Smell? Taste? Feel?

sticky cotton candy

bright sun

rainbow-colored rides

screaming and laughing

hot dogs

booming, thumping music

What's Happening PLOT

A story has a beginning, a middle, and an end. In the beginning, readers learn about the setting. They meet the characters. The middle is where most of the story happens. It holds the **plot**.

Toys come to life and go on crazy adventures.

A boy must prove a moose ate his homework, or he'll fail his class.

A wolf tries to blow down the houses of three little pigs.

BURP!

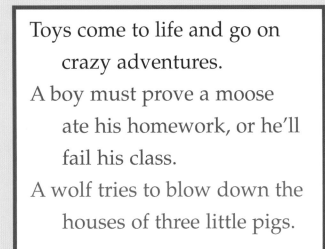

The end brings the story to a close.

plot—what happens in a story

Exercise

Choose one of the characters you created. Write about a time when things changed for him or her. For example, what if a turtle woke up and found its shell was missing?

What was life like for the character before this event?

What was it like after?

In the Moment SCENE

Scenes show important moments in a story. They use details to put readers in the action. Each scene moves the story toward the ending.

The barking got louder. I dashed across the yard. I saw a fence and jumped. The dog snapped at my shoe.

Exercise

Pick one of your characters. Write a scene about that character's very first bus ride. Start at pick up and stop at drop off. How does the bus look, smell, and feel? Is the character excited or scared? Describe the other riders. What does the driver's voice sound like?

I'm Feeling It MOOD

A story's **mood** is the way it makes readers feel. Some stories make readers feel sad or worried. Others make them smile. Use details to help set the mood.

The *gray* clouds *crept* across the sky. The flowers *froze*.

The *bright white* clouds *danced* across the sky. The flowers *laughed*.

Both examples are about clouds and flowers. But which example sounds happier? Why?

mood—a feeling

Look at this sentence—
The front door opened.

Now change it—
The newly painted door swung open.
The new sentence sets a **cheerful** mood.

Set a **scary** mood by changing the sentence again— **The heavy, dark door creaked open.**

Your turn! Try setting a sad mood and an *angry* mood.

What Did You Say? DIALOGUE

Dialogue gives your characters a voice. It helps tell a story. But it also shows what characters are like.

> "I am *not* going," Pete said. "No way!"
>
> "I guess you don't want dessert," his mom said.
>
> Pete thought. "Well, I'll go for a little bit."

This dialogue tells you Pete is stubborn. But he likes dessert too. And he's willing to change his mind to get some.

dialogue—words spoken between characters

Exercise

Write dialogue for two of your characters. Maybe they meet for the first time at a fall festival. One of them has hiccups. What do they say to one another? What do their words say about them?

FAST FACT

Quotation marks tell readers that a character is speaking. They appear around the words that the character says.

The End ENDINGS

Some stories end happily. Others don't. Some stories leave readers wanting more. Others tie up everything neatly. Write different endings, and see which one you like best.

Don't worry if your story isn't perfect right away. All writers **revise**. Maybe you need to add more details. Or maybe your dialogue doesn't sound quite right. Stories often get better when you revise.

**Everyone loves a good story.
Now go write one!**

revise—to change to make better

The End

Glossary

character (KAYR-ik-tur)—a person, animal, or creature in a story

detail (DEE-tayl)—one of many facts about a certain thing

dialogue (DYE-uh-lawg)—the words spoken between two or more characters

mood (MOOD)—the way that you are feeling

plot (PLOT)—what happens in a story

revise (ri-VIZE)—to change to make better or clearer

setting (SET-ting)—the time and place of a story

Read More

Bullard, Lisa. *You Can Write a Story!: A Story-Writing Recipe for Kids.* Minnetonka, Minn.: Two-Can, 2007.

Fandel, Jennifer. *You Can Write Cool Poems.* Mankato, Minn.: Capstone Press, 2012.

Loewen, Nancy. *Share a Scare: Writing Your Own Scary Story.* Writer's Toolbox. Minneapolis: Picture Window Books, 2009.

Internet Sites

FactHound offers a safe, fun way to find Internet sites related to this book. All of the sites on FactHound have been researched by our staff.

Here's all you do:

Visit *www.facthound.com*

Type in this code: 9781429676151

Super-cool stuff! Check out projects, games and lots more at
www.capstonekids.com

Index